The Clue

The focus in this book is on past tense verbs.

Verbs ending with -ed

looked wondered
jumped floated
landed pinned
bumped helped
pushed

Verbs ending with -ing

missing finding
following waiting
feeling

Bean was missing. Jelly had not seen him for two days. She had looked everywhere for him, but she could not find him.

She saw the little blue boat at the edge of the lake. There was something on the seat. Jelly wondered what it was.

It was a map of the lake with a path all round it. There was a cross by the big tree at the top of the lake. Hmmm?

Jelly woke him up. She made him stand up. He was wobbly on his legs. Jelly helped him back to the little blue boat.

They floated back across the lake. Wellington was waiting for them. Jelly pushed Bean onto Wellington's back.

They went back to their shed.
The vet came to see Bean and
soon he was feeling better.
Thank you, Jelly, for the rescue.

Words with digraphs used in this book

ay/ai:	days waiting
a-e:	lake same place made
ee/ea:	Bean seen seat tree see feeling
oa/ow:	boat arrows hollow following
o-e:	woke
oo:	soon
oo:	looked wood look
ou/ow:	round out found
or:	for
er:	better
ue:	blue clue rescue
aw:	saw